The Cheerleader's Guide

Guide

BY BARBARA EGBERT

Photos by Scott Smith and others

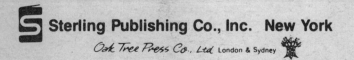

Sterling Publishing Co., Inc. New York

Oak Tree Press Co., Ltd London & Sydney

A Special School Book Fair, Inc. Edition

Adapted from Cheerleading and Songleading

Copyright © 1980 by Sterling Publishing Co., Inc.
Two Park Avenue, New York, N.Y. 10016
Distributed in Australia by Oak Tree Press Co., Ltd.,
P.O. Box J34, Brickfield Hill, Sydney 2000, N.S.W.
Distributed in the United Kingdom by Ward Lock Ltd.
116 Baker Street, London W.1
Manufactured in the United States of America
All rights reserved
Library of Congress Catalog Card No.: 80-52322
Sterling ISBN 0-8069-4626-1 Trade   Oak Tree 7061-2727-7
4627-X Library
8950-5 Paper

CONTENTS

PREFACE

Cheerleaders, songleaders, mascots, yell leaders, the drill team, pep club, marching band, and booster club: all of these people and groups contribute to school spirit and enthusiasm.

Late in the 19th century, students at Ivy League schools began cheering on their athletic teams with simple yells like "rah, rah, rah, sis boom yah." By the 1950s, cheerleading had reached the heights of popularity—matched only, perhaps, by the attention it is receiving today. Now, even our professional teams are cheered on by sideline squads. There are hundreds of cheerleading camps all over the country, and interest among high school students seems to increase all the time. More than ever before, men are becoming interested in cheerleading (they are often called yell leaders). The squads are becoming increasingly sophisticated, and the new gymnastic stunts, mounts, and pyramids are making the routines even more exciting.

CONDITIONING

A good performance begins with long, hard practice. The goals and talents of each squad will determine the frequency and length of the sessions. As a general rule, however, a squad should practice at least six hours a week. Break this practice time into three or four sessions of one-and-a-half to two hours.

A two-hour session is ideal because it allows adequate time for conditioning, stretching, choreography, and review of the cheers and routines. Sessions should be organized and conducted by a member of the squad. This person, called the "leader," should encourage new ideas and be willing to offer suggestions. Most important, she or he should project a positive attitude.

General Guidelines

Set up a schedule and stick to it, This way the squad members can plan their other activities around mandatory practice times. Use a large room for rehearsals. A dance studio with mirrors is a good place to work on routines and cheers.

Practice should begin promptly at the designated time. Latecomers will miss out on warm-ups and routine reviews, holding up the rest of the squad. It is impossible to develop a polished performance if squad members miss rehearsals or are consistently late.

Practice clothing should be non-confining and should give you room to stretch for kicks, splits, and jumps. Always begin rehearsals with a warm-up to prevent strained or pulled muscles.

Make good use of practice time. Chitchat can wait until after practice. Set up separate weekly meetings, if necessary, to discuss problems, disagreements, coming events, or evaluations of past performances. Periodically hold creativity sessions to encourage new ideas. It helps to listen to stimulating music when making up new steps or routines.

Squad members can give each other valuable feedback. Videotapes and game films give the squad members and the coach the opportunity to see the squad in action and to evaluate the performance for consistency in movement and style.

Practice Schedules

The leader should plan the rehearsals to make the best use of the allotted time. Here is a sample schedule. Allow for flexibility according to the progress of the members.

Minutes Activity

10-20	Warm-up: jog and body conditioning
10-20	Stretch for splits, kicks, jumps, stunts
10-20	Review of old material
20-40	Practice and perfection of new material
10	Review and evaluation
5-10	Discussion of future plans; equipment storage

Total: 1-2 hour practice session

Physical Conditioning

Cheerleading and songleading can be as strenuous as sports. The same rules of conditioning, weight control, performance technique, and physical training apply.

Conditioning refers to the preparedness of body and mind. Squad members should have sufficient strength and emotional control to meet performance demands, as well as the ability to perform at high levels of stress without physical and psychological fatigue. Proper conditioning is necessary for improved skill, agility, endurance, and self-confidence, and should be directed toward more efficient and effective performances. Increased strength allows for quicker, sharper movements and less muscle fatigue. Increased flexibility enlarges your range and variety of movement. Your kicks will be higher and your jump positions more extended. A running program should be included in the training sessions to increase cardiovascular endurance.

Warm-Up

Every practice session should begin with a warm-up, which protects against strains, muscle tears, muscle soreness, and injury.

✓ A warm-up raises body and deep-muscle temperature, which results in increased physical capacity.

✓ A warm-up strengthens ligaments and collagenous tissues, giving you more freedom of movement.

✓ A warm-up motivates you, especially if you listen to stimulating music with a strong dance beat.

Keep these rules in mind when you warm up:

✓ Begin slowly. Never make jerky or abrupt movements.

✓ Progress from a *general* body warm-up to a *specific* warm-up of specialized stretching.

✓ Work with large muscle groups first. Exercises should be simple and provide for movement of the entire body from head to toe.

✓ Don't overdo, or you will be too tired to perform well. On the other hand, if you don't warm up enough, you will not achieve optimum body temperature and you will not stretch your muscles properly.

Once squad members have learned the basics, they should mold the warm-up session to their individual needs. One person may need to spend more time stretching the legs for splits and another may want to spend more time on hamstring stretches.

Stretches

There are two ways to stretch, and each way has its proponents. In a *static stretch,* you hold a stretched position and lock the joints into a position that places the muscles and connective tissues at their greatest possible length. For example, to do a static stretch for the hamstrings, sit on the floor, extend your legs in front of you, and bend slowly from the waist forward to the toes and hold that position for several seconds. In a *ballistic stretch,* you bob and bounce. If you were touching your toes, you would bend over, touch your toes, and bob.

It has been found that the static stretch is just as effective as the ballistic method, and has several advantages. Most importantly, there is less danger of exceeding the stretching limits of the tissues, thereby reducing the possibility of muscle strains and injuries.

In a static stretch *for the hamstrings, sit on the floor, extend your legs in front of you, and bend slowly from the waist forward to the ankles or toes. Do not bob and bounce, as you would in* a ballistic stretch.

13

Warm-Up Exercises

Begin each practice with ten minutes of general conditioning and flexibility exercises. You can prepare yourself for these exercises with a three-to-four-minute jog. Warm up to music. It not only sets the mood for the practice and is psychologically motivating, but it also provides a constant beat to which you can perform the exercises.

The following exercises are designed for a total body warm-up.

Head Circles

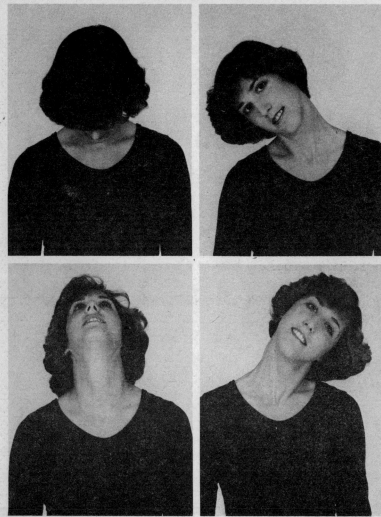

Slowly rotate your head forward, to the right, to the back, and to the left. Reverse and rotate in the opposite direction.

Shoulder Rolls

Relax your arms at your sides. Lift your shoulders upward and rotate them backwards. Reverse and rotate in a forward motion.

Rib Cage Isolations

Hold your arms parallel
to the floor or place them
on your hips. Push your
rib cage to the right, without moving your hips.
Push your rib cage to the
left. Repeat the sequence
several times.

Wrist Circles

Close your hands to form fists. Rotate them outward, then change direction and rotate them inward. Repeat several times.

Arm Circles

Hold your arms straight out in front of you. Swing them down at your sides and around above your head in a complete circle. Reverse.

Trunk Rotator

Place your hands on your hips. Bend forward at the waist. Rotate to the right, backwards, and to the left. Reverse.

19

Waist Stretch

Hold your arms parallel to the floor. Bend to the right, swinging your left arm to the right and over your head. Your right arm should swing in front of you to the left. Reverse.

Leg Stretch Series

Turn your body to the right and lunge (see the photos for the lunge position). Stretch your left calf muscle by pushing your left heel to the floor. Straighten your right leg and slowly bend from the waist so your torso touches your thigh. Hold the stretch for several seconds. Repeat the sequence with your right leg, then switch to your left side and go through the entire series again.

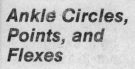

Ankle Circles, Points, and Flexes

Raise your right foot six inches from the floor and draw imaginary circles with your toes in an outward, then inward, direction. Then point your foot to the floor and flex it, drawing your toes inward toward you. Repeat, using your left foot.

Flexibility Exercises

Stretching exercises increase flexibility for splits and high kicks. There are two things to keep in mind. First, you must do these exercises at least once daily if they are going to be effective. Second, flexibility varies with each individual. Warm up and stretch at your own pace; do not push yourself too hard to attain one of these splits or kicks.

Hamstring Stretch, Sitting

Sit as shown, with your legs extended forward and your toes pointed. Bend forward, keeping your back straight and your head up. Push from the lower back. Hold the stretch for several seconds.
Variation: Sit, extend your legs, point your toes, and flex your feet toward your body. Slowly bend forward and hold.

Hamstring Stretch, Standing

Position your feet shoulder-width apart. Fold your arms and hold them straight out in front of you. Bend forward from the waist until you feel the tension in the back of your legs. Hold that position for several seconds and concentrate on relaxing your leg muscles. Return to an upright position and repeat the stretch on the right and then the left side. On these side stretches, hold your ankle and instep as pictured. Repeat the entire sequence twice.

Variation: Move your feet closer together and repeat the sequence. For the final stretch, bring your feet together, stretch forward, pull your head toward your knees, and hold until the muscle relaxes.

23

From a sitting position, lie back. Bring your legs straight over your head. Slowly bring them backwards, until you can touch the floor behind you with your toes. (Bring your legs back only as far as is comfortable.) Then bring your legs forward until you are in the sitting hamstring-stretch position.

Curl-Over

Frog Sit

Sit, as shown, with your feet together and your knees pointing outward. Put your hands on your feet. Bend forward, keeping your back straight, and hold for several seconds. Repeat three times. Place your hands on your knees and gently push them to the floor, then release. Repeat three times.

Lie on your back. Keep your left leg as straight as possible and slowly raise your right leg. Grab your right ankle with both hands and hold your leg in the stretched position for a few seconds. Then bend your leg at the knee and move your upper thigh slightly closer to your body. Straighten your leg and hold the position. Repeat three times and switch to your left leg.

Leg Stretch, Lying on Your Back

24

Side
Leg Raises
and Kicks

Lie on your left side, supporting your upper body with your left arm. (Bend your arm and rest on your elbow.) Raise your right leg toward your head. Grab your ankle with your right hand and hold the stretch. Keep your leg straight and point your foot. Lower your leg to the starting position and repeat five times. Repeat the entire sequence with your left leg.

Variation: Using the side position, hold your leg around the knee as shown. Alternately bend and straighten your leg.

Variation: Assume the side position and slowly kick your leg toward your head. Repeat five times and switch legs.

Spider Stretch

Squat on your right leg and extend your left leg straight to the side, as shown. Turn to the left, bend forward over your extended left leg, and hold. Move into the position shown. Then squat on your left leg, bend forward, and stretch over your right leg. Repeat three times.

Straddle Stretch

Sit on the floor with your legs straddled and toes pointed, as shown. Bring your hips forward and bend forward, keeping your back straight. Hold the forward stretch for several seconds. Then turn to the right side and bend forward so your upper body touches your thigh. Hold your ankle as shown. Hold the position for several seconds. Make the stretch to the left side. Repeat the sequence three times.

Hurdle Stretch

Sit on the floor. Extend your left leg in front of you and bend your right leg. Slowly bend forward over your left leg, keeping your back straight and your head up. Hold the position for several seconds. Stretch your upper left thigh as far back as you can. Lay back as shown. Repeat three times. Repeat the entire routine with your left leg.

Turning Split

Stand with your legs in a wide straddle. Lower your body toward the floor until you feel the maximum stretch. Gently turn your body to the right and sit in the splits. Push your body back into the centered position and slowly turn to the left. Support the split with your hands if necessary. Repeat several times.

Chair Split

Place two chairs (with the seats facing each other) about three feet apart. Spotters should hold the chairs to prevent them from slipping. Stand between the chairs. Place your hands on the seats and split your legs, supporting your weight with your hands. Lower your body until the stretch begins to feel uncomfortable and hold that position. Gradually lower your body each stretching session. Keep both legs straight and concentrate on contracting the muscles in back of your thighs. You have achieved a proper split when you can gradually lower your body to the floor, keeping your back upright, eyes forward, and legs straight. In the beginning, your back leg will touch the floor first. You should keep it strongly contracted throughout the split. Eventually, both your legs will touch the ground at the same time.

Kneeling Split

Kneel, placing your left knee on the floor. Bend forward so your upper body touches your right thigh. Push your right leg forward until you are in a complete split. Stretch until the position begins to feel uncomfortable. Hold the stretch. You should place your feet and legs on an imaginary straight line and point both feet. Repeat with your left leg.

Wall Split

Stand with your back against a wall, hands to your sides and against the wall for support. A partner should stand in front of you facing the wall. Lift your left leg forward to waist level, allowing your partner to grab it at the ankle with both hands. Push your leg downward for one second as your partner resists. Relax the muscle as your partner raises the leg several inches higher. Contract and push it against your partner's resisting hands. Relax as your partner raises your leg several inches again. Continue in this way until your leg is in a maximum stretch. Slowly lower your leg. Repeat the exercise with your left leg.

In Review

✓ Conditioning, weight control, performance technique, and physical training are as important to cheerleading as they are to sports.

✓ Set up a practice schedule and stick to it.

✓ Wear non-confining clothing when you practice.

✓ Begin practice sessions with a thorough warm-up.

✓ A good warm-up includes exercises for the entire body.

✓ For increased flexibility, do a series of stretching exercises every day.

CHEERLEADING

Cheerleaders have one job: to encourage the crowd to support the team. In order to do this, a good cheerleader develops a professional approach to the performance, projects a positive attitude to the crowd, and sets an example of good sportsmanship.

Crowd Control

The spectators came to watch the game. It is your job as a cheerleader to direct that interest toward the support of your team. There are many ways to do this, and to maintain good sportsmanship at the same time.

✓ Use positive cheers and chants; don't use cheers and chants that will create friction between factions in the crowd.

✓ Meet with the visiting team's cheerleaders before the game and plan the use of time-outs for cheers, giving each cheering squad an equal opportunity to perform. Do not cheer when the cheering squad for the opposing team is doing a cheer or routine.

✓ Don't let the crowd make catcalls and other noise during periods of concentration, such as during a free throw in a basketball game.

✓ Respect the officials' and referees' decisions.

✓ Relate cheers to the game situation. For example, coach the crowd to yell an encouraging chant as soon as the team comes out of the huddle to attempt a crucial score.

✓ Let the fans know that their support is crucial to the outcome of the game. Thank them for their support by performing a special cheer or chant for them after the game. If possible, occasionally move into the bleachers to encourage greater cheering support.

✓ Get the crowd involved with cheering contests between different groups: freshmen vs. seniors, students vs. teachers, and so on.

✓ If booing or other negative outbursts begin, signal the troublemakers to stop. If the disturbance becomes louder, divert the crowd's attention by starting a cheer. Try to involve small negative factions by

Your job as a cheerleader is to communicate with the crowd— vocally, as well as with arm, leg, and body motions.

getting them to cheer with you, instead of independently. (It may be helpful to talk to the leader of the group during a break in the game.)

Crowd Communication

Your voice is your most important means of communication. Take care of it! Strength, clarity, and tone are the signs of a well-trained voice. *Don't* yell or scream in a high-pitched voice; *do* articulate your words clearly with the proper inflection and avoid monotones. Use your diaphragm for voice projection.

Use a megaphone to develop contact with the crowd. Use it to yell encouragement to the players and instructions to the crowd. Don't use it to shout disapproval over an official's call or to yell at opposing players or cheerleaders. Don't lend your megaphone to fans in the bleachers.

In a football stadium, use a microphone to keep in touch with the large crowd. Have a pregame sound check and make sure the speakers are directed to all sections of the crowd.

Control the crowd's cheers with visual and vocal cues. Use visual cues to indicate the length of the chants; by holding up one finger, you can tell the fans to repeat the chant one more time. You can do the same thing with vocal cues, simply by saying "One more time." You can also use vocal cues as starting signals, such as "Ready? Go!" and to elicit a better response, such as "Louder!"

Develop a strong, clear voice. Use your diaphragm for projection. Most important, talk to, don't scream at, the audience. Cheerleaders often use megaphones, and in large stadiums they use microphones.

Chants

Chants are supportive yells in which the crowd participates. At pep rallies before the game, run through your repertoire of chants with the students. Then, when you give them the signal during the game, they will be able to launch right into the chant you indicate. See pages 77-107 for some typical chants.

Sometimes, you will be able to give a short introduction to a chant. This will enable you to encourage the crowd and to explain why a chant is necessary. For example, you might say, "Come on, let's hear it. We've got ten yards to go to tie up the game." Basketball moves so quickly you probably won't have time to give introductions; you will have time during football games, however.

Here are some tips to make your chants more effective:

✓ Maintain a strong and consistent rhythm.

✓ Control the tempo at all times.

✓ Use special effects: big buildups, loud vs. soft inflections, slow vs. fast tempo.

✓ Use the band and taped music for different effects.

✓ Use simple, precise movements for emphasis.

When to Chant	*When Not to Chant*
Football	
Pregame	Team is at the line of scrimage
Time-outs	age
Halftime	Play is in progress
When team is huddled	Signals are being called
At end of a play	
After scores	
Encouragement for injured	
Basketball	
Same as above	Shooting free throws
Additions:	During controversial play
During plays	Player injured (unless for
Jump balls	encouragement)

37

Cheers

Cheers, as opposed to chants, are performed only by the cheerleaders. Often, they are longer than chants. Cheers are a form of entertainment and a means of stimulating the audience to support the team. See pages 77-107 for typical cheers.

Follow these steps in learning a cheer:

✓ Learn the words and the rhythm, paying attention to what words receive the emphasis.

✓ Learn motions to coincide with each word; break down the motions and perfect each one.

✓ Incorporate formations, mounts, and stunts to go with the ending words of a cheer. The last word of a cheer should match the final motion or mount. Incorporate complicated moves, such as cartwheels, mounts, and tumbling stunts, but only when the squad members have mastered them.

✓ Put the entire cheer together and practice the correct tempo (timing).

✓ Critique the cheer. Look for sharp motions. Are you holding your arms at the right angle and on the right level? Is the tempo consistent throughout the cheer? Are you executing your mounts, formations, and ending poses properly? Are you making eye contact with the fans and projecting enthusiasm?

Constructing Your Cheers

You will construct your cheerleading routines out of hand, arm, and leg motions orchestrated to the words of the cheers. How you put the movements together to match the words of the cheers is your decision. There are, however, basic cheerleading moves that you will incorporate in your cheers.

The style of cheerleading you are probably most used

38

Block-style cheerleading motions feature rigid, sharp arm movements at angles of 45, 90 and 180 degrees, and blades, which are formed by straight hands and extended fingers. Block is the style most cheerleaders use.

Boogie-style cheerleading is loose in form and features flowing, dancelike steps and relaxed arm and body movements.

Concentrate on keeping your arms as straight as possible and at the proper angles. Here, each member of the squad holds her arms at a 90-degree angle.

Plan every move in your cheerleading routine. Nothing should just happen; all movements should be coordinated. These cheerleaders have placed their hands on their hips in the same way and are bending at their waists to the same degree. The effect: a smooth, graceful, eyepleasing routine.

40

Actions, words, and facial expressions are the tricks of a cheerleader's trade. The mark of a polished cheerleader is the ability to put these elements together. A smile, or even an anxious look, combined with the right words and movements, can tell the whole story: GO! PUT IT IN! PUSH 'EM BACK.

to seeing is called *block style*. This style features precise arm movements at angles of 45, 90, and 180 degrees, blades (where you hold your hands straight and extend your fingers in bladelike fashion), leg lunges, and clenched fists.

When to Cheer	*When Not to Cheer*
Football	
Pregame	Team is at the line of scrim-
Time-outs	mage
Halftime	Play is in progress
When team is huddled	Signals are being called
At end of a play	
After scores	
Basketball	
Time-outs	Shooting free throws
Pregame	During playing time
Halftime	
(when floor is cleared and	
there is a break in the action	
play)	

The Game Plan

Discuss your plan for the game with the songleaders and the other spirit squads. Assign different times in the game to the different squads. For example, give the first time-out to the cheerleaders, the second time-out to the songleaders, the third time-out to the visiting cheerleaders, and so on.

Communicate with the other squads during the game. Use visual signals or announce through your megaphone when you are going to begin a cheer or routine. This way, the other squads can join you or do a complementary routine. Songleaders often join the cheerleaders in cheers and chants.

A squad leader, or captain, should give the signal to start a cheer. A different squad member can act as leader for each game. The important thing is, one person must be in charge of initiating the cheers. The other cheerleaders will spread themselves out in front of the crowd and watch the leader for their cues.

Follow these general rules in planning your performance:

✓Prior to the game, make a game plan of cheers for time-outs, half-time, and pregame and post-game proceedings. Make sure all squad members are familiar with the schedule.

✓Be ready physically and mentally. Know the game plan and your individual responsibilities. Be on the court or field 10 minutes before the game begins.

✓Pay attention to the game. Avoid unnecessary conversation with other cheerleaders.

✓Let the game situation (kickoffs, huddles, time-outs) determine which cheers and chants you use.

✓Anticipate game actions and set up appropriate cheers. Watch the officials, scoreboard, and timer to keep up with the action.

✓Watch for quick situation changes (fumbles, interceptions, turnovers, penalties).

✓Do not use a chant for every game situation, only key plays.

✓After a cheer, rush to (move quickly toward) the crowd and begin a short, rousing chant.

✓Initiate a chant after a spectacular play when the crowd is excited.

✓Wear a minimum of jewelry; do not chew gum.

Cheerleading Repertoire

Type	Description
Chants	Short, one or two line yells
Crowd Repeat Chants	Chants that crowd will repeat after cheer squad line by line; cheerleaders may also ask crowd for specific responses or answers to questions
Welcome Cheer	Cheer performed by the squad to welcome the opposing school's crowd
Short Cheers	Three- to seven-line cheers
Long Cheers	Over seven lines long
Cheer/Song Routines	Cheerleaders and songleaders combine squads in the form of a dance/cheer routine. Chants, stunts are included along with dance

Purpose	Other
Increase crowd involvement and team support	Repeat three to four times
Crowd participation	Coach the fans before trying a repeat chant and explain when and what they are to respond
To greet the opposing crowd and introduce cheer squad	Demonstrates sportsmanship
For time-outs; should be short, snappy and eye-catching to increase audience pep	Ideal when performing before a large crowd
Used most often for haltime entertainment; gives opportunity to use spectacular stunts and mounts	More effective with small and close crowd (can understand the words)
Shows unity of spirit squads; provides variety in entertainment	Gymnastics can also be performed

Jumps

Jumps are probably the most popular of all cheer-leading moves. They are fun to do and exciting to watch—provided, of course, you do them properly. Most jumps begin with this three-step approach:

Start, as shown, with your arms up in a V and step forward, crossing your arms in front of you.

Do a small hop, bringing your feet together and swinging your arms back.

Jump into the final jump pose, swinging your arms back to the position shown.

You can add a variety of arm and leg poses to the final step of the jump. *Remember:* Always point your toes when you are executing these jump positions and land with your knees bent to absorb the shock.

Herkie

Kick one leg straight out in front of you, parallel to the floor. Kick the other leg behind you, bending it at the knee. You can punch one arm in the air and place the other one on your waist, or you can extend both your arms out at your sides.

Bambi

Bend one leg at the knee and lift it in front of you. Kick your other leg straight out behind you. Extend your arms straight out at your sides, parallel to the floor. Hold your hands in the blades position.

Reindeer

Hold your legs in the same position you used for the Bambi. Extend your arms above your head. Hold them as close to your ears as possible.

Banana

Extend your arms above your head and hold them as close to your ears as possible. Hold your hands in blades. Arch your back slightly and kick your feet back, keeping your legs straight.

Tuck

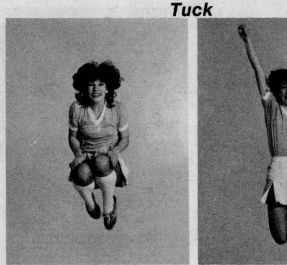

In the basic tuck motion, you bring your knees up to your chest in a tight tuck. Vary the jump with different arm movements.

In the *slap tuck,* hit your thighs as you are tucking your legs and extend your arms over your head.

In the *motion tuck,* swing your arms up as you tuck your legs. Bring your arms in a complete circle behind you. Then, clenching your fists, bring your hands straight out in front of you at the conclusion of the jump.

In a *simple tuck,* touch your hands under your tucked knees at the height of the jump.

Spread Eagle

Kick your legs to the side in a straddle position and bring your arms over your head in a V formation. Hold your arms as close to your ears as possible.

Stag

Kick one leg to the side, pointing your toes. Tuck the other leg, bringing the foot as close to your knee as possible. Extend your arms at your sides.

Side C

Face sideways. Form a box with your arms over your head. Kick your feet up to the back and bring them in toward your thighs, forming an arc. Hold your head toward the audience as shown.

Hurdler

Kick your front leg up as if you were doing a high kick. Bend your back leg as shown. You can keep your arms at your sides or you can reach forward to touch your right foot during the kick.

Pike

Raise your legs straight out in front of you parallel to the floor. Reach for your toes.

Back Arch

Kick your legs up and back. Bring your arms back, trying to touch your toes with your elbows. Face sideways and turn your head toward the crowd when you do this jump. This way, they can see the arch in your back.

Double Nine

Kick forward and up with one leg and tuck the other leg in, touching your opposite knee with your foot. Your legs will form a nine. Hold your hands in a similar position, creating the second nine.

Partner Stunts

Partner stunts add flair, variety, and a touch of the dramatic to a routine. With practice, any member of the squad should be able to master these complex mounts. You'll soon learn that timing and balance are the most important ingredients.

Base Positions

To maintain a proper base position, give yourself a wide base of support and a low center of gravity. The more area you give your partner to step into, the easier the mount will be. In most mounts, your partner will step into the *pocket, which is the area at the top of the thigh formed by a lunge.*

The three base positions most commonly used are the *forward lunge,* the *side lunge,* and the *ready position.*

Forward Lunge

Take a step forward, putting your body weight on your bent front leg. Keep your back leg straight.

Side Lunge

Hold one leg out to one side and bend it at the knee. Extend your other leg to the other side. Spread your feet as far apart as possible. This way you will form a fairly flat table with your bent leg onto which your partner can step. Center your body weight over your bent leg.

Ready Position

Stand with your feet shoulder-width apart and flex your knees slightly. Bend forward at your hips. Put your hands on your knees, holding your arms straight. Keep your back as straight as you can. It should form a flat table for mounting.

Use these base positions to perform a variety of mounts. Remember, let spotters help you climb into and out of mounts during practices.

Pony Mount Sit

Base Assume the ready position.

Mount Place one hand on the base's neck and your other hand on the base's lower back. Push down on these points, then jump up and sit, as shown, on the base's back. Tuck your legs back and extend your arms to the side or above your head.

Pony Mount Kneel

Base Assume the ready position.

Mount Follow the same instructions for the Pony Mount Sit, only jump higher so you land on the base's back on your knees.

Pony Mount Stand

Base Assume the ready position.
Mount Run toward the base. Push off the base's lower back with both hands and jump up into a standing position.

Walk Up to Back Knee Stand

Base Step into the forward lunge position and clasp your hands behind your lower back.

Mount Place one foot in the handhold and step up. Bend the other leg at the knee and rest it on the base's shoulder.

Side Thigh Sit

Base   Do a side lunge and hold the mount around the waist.

Mount   Stand to the front of the base and place your inside arm around the base's shoulders. Place your inside ankle in the pocket. Take a small jump and assume a sitting position on the base's thigh.

Base   Help the mount assume a sitting position.

Side-Thigh   L Catch

Base   Do a side lunge.

Mount   Stand to the front of the base and place your inside ankle in the pocket.

Base   Place one arm around the mount's waist.

Mount   Hold the base around the neck. Kick your outside leg toward the base.

Base   Catch the mount's leg and hold it by the ankle.

Side Thigh Stand

Base Lunge to the side.
Mount Stand behind the base and place your inside foot in the pocket.
Base Wrap your arm around the upper portion of the mount's knee. Draw the mount's leg close to your body.
Mount Extend your inside leg and bring your other leg up to complete the stand. Hold your hands and arms in one of the positions pictured.

L Stand

Base Lunge to the side.
Mount Place your outside leg in the pocket.
Base Wrap your arm around the mount's outside leg.
Mount Step up, placing your body weight on the outside leg. Swing your other leg up to rest on the base's shoulder.
Base Hold the mount's leg by the ankle. Lift if off your shoulder and raise it upward.
Mount Position your arms in an L, one parallel to the floor and one parallel to your outside leg.

Front Thigh Stand

Mount Stand with your back to the base.

Base Put yourself in a position similar to the ready position, forming a table with your thighs. Put your hands on the mount's waist.

Mount Hold onto the base's wrists and jump to the front of the base's thighs.

Base Lift the mount into position on your thighs.

Mount Place your feet in a pigeon-toed position in the pockets and gradually begin to stand.

Base Move your hands to the mount's upper thighs and gradually lean the mount forward until your arms are locked. Lean backwards to maintain stability.

Face-to-Face Front Thigh Stand

Mount and Base Face each other and pretend to shake hands, right hand to right hand and left hand to left hand, but clasp each other's wrists. *Mount* Place your feet on the base's thighs one at a time and stand straight up.

Mount and Base Gradually lean back until your arms are straight. Release one set of hands and extend your arms as shown.

Flying Angel

Base Assume the side lunge position. Flex your knees and form a circle with your arms.

Mount Run from the side toward the base and jump so you land in the base's arms, with one leg bent inside the circle and the other leg extended to the side. Point your toes.

Base Catch the mount as shown.

Mount Extend your arms to the sides.

Back Angel

Base Stand behind the mount. Position your hands on the mount's buttocks.

Mount Jump.

Base Lift the mount during the jump until the overhead pose is completed. Extend your arms fully.

Mount Arch your back and bend your knee.

Base For the dismount, lift the mount back to the floor.

63

Walk-Up to Shoulder Sit

Base Stand in a side lunge.
Mount Stand to the rear and side of the base. Clasp the base's hands and place your outside leg in the pocket. Step onto the base's thigh and swing your other leg over the base's other shoulder.

Sit with your weight centered on both shoulders and extend your arms.

Variation: Do not grasp the base's hands. Instead, put your hands onto the base's shoulders and swing into position.

Shoulder Sit into Rear Dismount

Mount   To dismount to the front, hold onto the base's hands (which are positioned on the outside of your legs). Pop over the base's head.

Base   Push the mount up and over your head.

Mount   Hold the base's hands between your straddled legs as shown.

Base   On signal, push the mount up and off your shoulders.
Mount   Land on your feet to the rear of the base.

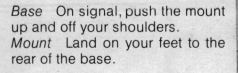

Walk-Up
to Shoulder
Stand

Base and Mount Face each
other and shake hands, right
to right and left to left.

Mount Step into the pocket
with the outside leg.

Mount Step onto the base's
opposite shoulder with your
leg, then step onto the other
shoulder with your outside leg.

Hold the base's hands as pictured for support.

Once you have gotten into the final position, extend your arms. *Base* Assist the mount into the proper position. Hold the mount below the knees for support.

Mount To dismount, hold the base's hands and jump forward.

Side Lift

Base Place your left hand on the mount's waist and your right hand on the mount's leg as shown. Lift the mount overhead, extending your arms fully.

Mount Jump as the base begins to lift you overhead.

Around-the-World

Base Hold the mount in your arms as shown. Swing the mount to the right. Release the mount's leg, and hold your right arm around the mount's back.

Mount Keep your legs fully extended while they swing around behind the base. Hold your left arm around the base's neck.

Base Turn to the right and pick up the mount's legs behind the knees.

Mount Flex at your knees and free your grasp of the base's neck. Do a sit-up so you bring your torso into the base's right arm.

Base Lift with your left arm to help the mount into the proper ending position.

End the stunt in exactly the same postion in which you started it.

Split Catch

This stunt calls for two bases and one mount.
Bases Position yourselves so one of you is slightly behind the other.
Mount Step between the bases and grab their outside hands. At a predetermined signal, jump into a split.
Bases During the jump into a split, lift the mount onto your shoulders by pulling up with your outside hands.

Flip-Over

Mount Stand one step behind and to the right of the base. Kick forward and up with your right leg.

Base Reach behind to the mount's lower back with your right arm and pull the mount onto your right shoulder. Use your left arm for extra support.

Mount and Base Extend your arms parallel to the floor.

Mount To dismount, grab the base's left hand with your left hand, tuck your head, and do a flip across the front of the base's body.

Base With your right hand, support the mount's back during the flip.

Cheek-to-Cheek

Base and Mount Face each other.

Mount Put your arms around the base's neck.

Base Grab the mount's waist.

Mount Jump up and straddle the base's torso as pictured.

Base Bend at the waist. Then, stand upright and lift the mount into a handstand position on your shoulders.

Tumbling

You can embellish these stunts with tumbling techniques, such as cartwheels, roundoffs, forward rolls, and
front and back walkovers. Master these stunts thoroughly before you incorporate them into your cheers. If your
squad is not adept at tumbling, don't attempt to do
them. Most schools offer tumbling and gymnastic
classes; take advantage of them.

Cheerleaders frequently use cartwheels—usually as
they run onto or off of the court or field and after a cheer.
To do a cartwheel, lift your arms over your head and lift
your left leg. Step forward on your left foot and place
your left hand on the floor directly in front of your body.
Swing your right leg upward and push off with your left
leg. Bring your left leg up so your legs are astraddle in
the air. Place your right hand on the floor directly in
front of the left hand. Your right leg will contact the floor
first. Flex it, bring your left down, and assume an
upright position.

Pyramids

Combine mounts and stunts to create pyramids. These illustrations will give you ideas for many different types. Study them for the various mounts and stunts, then practice. Always use spotters until you have perfected the pyramids. When you feel comfortable doing them, include them in your cheers. Remember to allow ample time during the cheer to position the mounts without slowing the beat, and make sure the final pose corresponds with the ending word of the cheer.

Cheers and Chants

Now that you know the various cheerleading movements, you can start thinking about combining your actions with the words of the cheers and chants. The rule of thumb is: *your motions should emphasize the words of the cheer.* Lunge or punch the air on words like FIGHT; throw your hands up or jump forward on words like GO. Here are typical cheers and chants for basketball and football games. Study them, thinking about how you can match them with the proper movements.

Key to Cheers and Chants

X means clap.

... means continue with the single word: Go, go, go, ...

S-C-O-R-E means spell out each letter of the word.

S-C-OR-E means the letters OR are said quickly together on the same beat.

Hold THAT line means capitalized words receive the accent.

X-X means there is a pause between claps.

Basketball: Offensive Chants

Put it in, put it in XX
Right in!

T-E-A-M
Teamwork, Teamwork

Do it, do it X
All right!

XX XXX XXXX
Let's go!

Harder, harder
Try a little harder

Let's get fired up XX XXX

We want TWO

HUS-TLE
Hustle, hustle

Break that tie, hey!

Raise that score X
Raise that score

Work it in XX

Put it in XX

More, more, raise that score!

We want XX
Two points XX

S-C-ORE score more

Take it down, put it in
Come on Lions, let's win

Take it down, put it through
Come on Lions, it's up to you

Look alive, big five XX
Let's drive

More, more, raise that score!

Move it, move it, right now
M-O-V-E, move it now!

(For a jump ball situation)
Jump, jump, higher, higher
Jump, jump, jump
Jump, Tigers, jump
Get that ball and GO

Bears X, Bears X
Go for two!

Pull yourself together team
And work it, work it,
Work it out!

Take it easy, take it slow
Come on, let's go!

2 points, 2 points
Score, score!

R-I-M
Thru the rim, thru the rim

Set it up team, pour on the steam, hey!

You can do it XX
So get to it XX

M-O-V-E
Move it, move it

Move it, move it
Down, down that floor X, score

Look alive, mighty five, look alive XX

Don't give up,
Don't let it get you down

Basket XX
2 points XX

Looking good, big team,
You're looking good

You can do it, sure you can

Basketball: Defensive Chants

Get that ball and go, go
Get that ball and GO

Pressure, defense
Pressure XX

Hey, attack
Get that ball back!

Take it away

Take, take
Take it away

De-fense, de-fense
Get tough

Fight, fight X
Fight harder

T-A-K-E
Take it X away

Guard your man, guard your man
Don't let him shoot!

Get tough, get tough, XX XX

Defense, defense XX XXX

Steal it, steal it

We want the ball to go that-a-way, that-a-way

Football: Offensive Chants

Victory for varsity,
Hey, let's go

Go Redskins, GO

Let's go XX, right now XX

Go, go, go, go, . . .

Score, score, score, . . .

Down the field, down the field,
Don't stop!

Go, go, go, go,
Go for it, go for it

We want a big first down!

It's touchdown time, we're movin'
Groovin' down, down the line XX

T-O-U-C-H down
Touchdown

T-O-U-CH
Touchdown

O-S-U
Move it, move it, move it

Move it, move it X
Right now!

S-C-OR-E
Score 6 points

We're movin' for XX
A big score!

Football: Defensive Chants

Hold 'em defense,
Hold 'em XX

Hold 'em defense,
Hold 'em defense,
Hey, hey, hey

Hold that line X
Hey, hold that line X

Push 'em back, push 'em back,
Way back!

Defense Lions, defense

Defensive line X
Get 'em get 'em get 'em X

De-fense, de-fense X
Get tough

Pressure, defense
Pressure XX

Defense, defense,
Dig right in!

Block that kick,
Hey, block that kick

Hold 'em, hold 'em, . . .

Get tough, get tough, XX XX

Hold that line X

Hold X that line X

De-fense,
Push 'em way back!

Fight, fight,
Fight harder!

Sideline Chants

We're crazy, that's what I said
We're crazy, gonna knock 'em dead
We're C-R-A-Z-Y, are we so crazy,
That's what I said
We're crazy, gonna knock 'em dead
We're C-R-A-Z-Y, are we so crazy?

Get down, get funky, get loose
And groove to the beat
Get your body movin' and start with the feet
Go feet 2, 3, 4
Go knees 2, 3, 4
Go hips 2, 3, 4
Go arms 2, 3, 4
Go shoulders 2, 3, 4
That's it! Get down, get funky, get loose!

Rock X-X, steady X-X
'Cause your team X
Ain't even ready X-X
Rock, rock, rock, rock
Steady, eady, eady, eady
(Repeat entire chant) ROCK!

Bulldogs,
Don't take no ump, jive
Bulldogs,
We are Alive!

Got our minds made up
Come on, we can win it
Win it team, anytime
Say, "Wooo"

Fired up and ready,
Our team is alive
Let's go-go, go-go

Fire up!
For a victory!

E-A-S-Y
You can do it
If you give it a try
It's easy X hey, hey
It's easy XXX

Shine through XXX

Superman, Macho Man
Match our team if you can

Freak X out X
The other team X

I say get, I say get it,
I say get it on, get it on, get it on, OOH!

Sock it, sock it, sock it to 'em, NOW!

That's the way, uh huh, uh huh, we like it!

Our spirit XX, our spirit is high
If you hear it XX then please reply

You gotta want it, to win it
And we want it more!

We've got the fever, we're hot
We can't be stopped!

Boy, are we enthusiastic
We are feeling G-O-OD

Let's get a little bit rowdy
R-O-W-AD-Y

P.H.S. can you dig it
Everybody's here
So everybody cheer!

(Other team) is dynamite,
Let's put their fuses out!

Cougar power! Cougar power!

Aah, but you can bet,
You ain't seen nothin' yet

We've got pride on our side
You know it, we show it!

Anywhere we meet you
We know we're gonna beat you
Any T-I-M-E time

1, 2, 3-4-5, Tigers don't take no jive
6, 7, 8-9-10, Tigers gonna do it again

We're rowdy, we're rough
We're big and mean and tough
We're rowdy, rough, big and tough
I say we're rough and tough

Here we go Tigers, here we go XX

Gators are dynamite, all right!

Come on Chargers, we gotta go,
We gotta go, we gotta go

Tiger XX Power XX

We are dynamite
You don't mess with dynamite

We've got what it takes
To make our team
Super Great!

Aaah—Boom—Boom
We're gonna rock this room
To a soul tune
To get 2—To get 2
Aaah—Bam—Bam
We're gonna really jam
And not take no jive
From the Eagle five
We'll get 2—We'll get 2
Aaah—Boom—Boom
We're gonna really zoom
All around the floor
We'll beat you—We'll beat you
YEAH!

We are the Eagles
Oh yeah the very best
And when we move X X
We just can't lose
Oh yeah and when we're hot X X
We can't be stopped
We are the Eagle team
Oh yeah we're big and mean
And when we move X X
We just can't lose
Oh yeah and when we're hot X X
We can't be stopped

Cheers

We're gonna get you yet
On that you can bet
Sooo, Eagles, Get Set!

L.A. Stars are we
Our aim is victory
A goal so high
We reach for the sky
Stars—Fly High!

Onward to Victory
The time is now at hand
So onward to victory
We've made our winning stand
(pause) Onward

The Trojans are coming
We'll get you in the end
The Trojans are coming
You can bet we're gonna win
Trojans Win Again

We've got it
It's here to stay
We feel it
And *(opponents)* can't take it away
We've got it *(pause)*
We feel it (XX)
It's *(mascot)* Spirit

We've got a team that's really F-I-N-E fine,
And anytime we meet you
We'll be sure to beat you
Any T-I-M-E, T-I-M-E time!

Cougars, fight
Show your might
Cougars want a victory
Win, tonight

Get ready, get set
The Cougar team is The best yet
Get ready, get set

We're out X to shout about
A team that has no doubt
We're on the move,
We're gonna groove
So, hey, watch out!

Hustle, get tough
We're gonna run and gun
Till they've had enough
Hustle, hustle
A-get-tough

Stepping out into action
Stepping out with might
F-I-G-H-T, Fight

Get started, don't stop
Tigers on top
F-I-G-H-T
Tigers on top

Shock, surprise!
Eagles best be wise
You better get back, get back
Get out of our way
You better get back, get back
'Cause this just ain't your day

Go, go-go, GOOOO go
We're ready
The Royals are about to begin
So go Royals, WIN

We've gotcha, hey, you
You better beware
Cause we've gotcha
We're everywhere
There's no turning back now
'Cause . . . . We've gotcha

Don't give in, don't give up
Just take the score higher up
Take it up, hey *(repeat 3 times)*
Take it up, up, up
Take it up, hey *(repeat 3 times)*
Take it up, up, UP

S XXX U XXX C XXX C XXX E XXX S XXX
   S XXX
S-U-C-C-E-S-S
That's the way we spell success
We wish you luck and all the rest
With S-U-C-C-E-S-S, Success

Get your act together now!
Get your act together,
The Suns team is better
And we're getting down on you

Boogie, boogie, boogie
Mighty Royals, get down
(Repeat)
We'll boogie down
We'll boogie through
We'll boogie right on over you
Boogie, boogie, boogie
Mighty Royals, get down
Boogie, boogie, boogie
Mighty Royals, GET DOWN

Gotta get it together
Gotta fight X
Come on let's do it
Gotta get it together
Gotta W-I-N win
Let's get it together and win

Jump out, shout it out
Jump in, gonna win, hey
AHHH *(four beats)*
Watch the way we go—GO
Watch the way we fight—FIGHT
Watch the way we win—WIN
Win this game tonight

Defense, Longhorns
Hold on tight XX
Let's fight

We've got the style
And we've got the beat
You just sit right down
And watch us compete

Power beat, rockin' beat
And for us it's a victory
V-I-C-T-O-R-Y, Powerbeat!

YOU gotta get on down
Gotta strut your stuff
Get tough!

It's you big team
That we're yelling for
So win this game
With another score
S-C-O-R-E Score!

It's up to you
So do what you gotta do
You gotta S-C-O-R-E
Score for a victory

Eagles . . . got power
They're in the victory hour
So ease off . . . jump back . . . .
We're on the winning track

Hip Hip Hurrah for Mr. Dyno
Hi hip Hurrah for Mr. D
He can run and he can throw
Give him the ball and just look at him go
Hip hip hurrah for Mr. Dyno
Hip hip hurrah for Mr. D
We'll give a great big cheer
For the hero of the year
Mr. Dyno, Southwest High

Zip, hey
Zap, hey
A-zoom-zow
Flash more points
On the scoreboard now
Zip, hey
Zap, hey
A-Zoom-Zow

Together we'll fight
Together we'll win
Trojans, victorious
Never give in!

Suns are hot
And can't be stopped
We'll take you round and round
We'll take you up and down
And Suns XX are hot

Gotta get it together
Gotta fight! (X)
C'mon let's do it
Gotta get it together
Gotta F-I-G-H-T
FIGHT!

Crowd Repeat Chants

The words with the parentheses ( ) are the words the crowd will repeat.

Hey (hey), Hey (hey)
Tigers want a victory, Hey (hey)
What you get is what you see, Hey (hey)
We get down when we attack, Hey (hey)
We ain't holding nothing back, Hey (hey)
Hey (hey), Hey (hey) HEY!

Cougars gonna play a team that's tough
Gonna rack them up and strut their stuff
Said what (said Cougars)
Said who (the Cougars)
Cougars gonna be too hot to trot
Cougars gonna be too hot to stop
Said what (said Cougars)
Said who (the Cougars)

Hey, Crowd (yeah)
Hey, Crowd (yeah)
Introduce yourself (right on)
(We are the crowd) Yeah
(And we are proud) Yeah
(That's why we yell) Yeah
(So very loud) Yeah

Hey, crowd (yeah)
Hey, crowd (yeah)
Let me see you get down (no way)
Let me see you get down (OK)
D-O-W-N, that's the way we get down
D-O-W-N, that's the way we get down

We (we), the Lions (the Lions)
We (we), will swoop (swoop)
We (we), the Lions (the Lions)
We (we), will take you to the hoop (woosh)

Countdown (5, 4)
Knock it on down (3, 2)
All the way down (5, 4, 3, 2)
X We're number one
We're number 1, 'cause number 2 won't do (*Crowd repeats*)
We're number ONE!

Are you ready? (yeah)
Are you ready (yeah)
Get down 2, 3, 4 *(Crowd repeats)*
Always talking 'bout what you're going to do *(Crowd repeats)*
Eagles gonna do it too *(Crowd repeats)*
You say you're gonna do your thing *(Crowd repeats)*
Eagles gonna win this game *(Crowd repeats)*
Tell me if I'm right (you're right)
Correct me if I'm wrong (you're right)

Sock X it X, sock it to me Royals *(Crowd repeats)*
Sock it X to ME X, sock it to me Royals *(Crowd repeats)*
Sock it to me ma, ma, ma-ma-ma-Royals *(Crowd Repeats)*
Sock it to me ma, ma, ma-ma-ma-Royals, Sock it to me ma, ma-ma, Hey *(Crowd repeats)*

Hey X we're here X to do a get-down cheer *(Crowd repeats)*
Clap X your hands X boogie with the band *(Crowd repeats)*
Lean it to the left *(Crowd repeats)*
Rock on to the right *(Crowd repeats)*
Boogie on down *(Crowd repeats)*
'Cause we're the best around *(Crowd repeats)*
Hey, X we're here X to do a get-down cheer *(Crowd repeats)*
Hey, we're here!

Our team is what? (Red Hot!)
Our team is R-E-D
With a little bit of H-O-T
Our team is what? (Red Hot!)

Don't fool with the Kool, 'Cause the cool don't fool
 (Crowd repeats)
Don't mess with the best, 'cause the best don't mess
 (Crowd repeats)
So be cool you fool, don't tangle with the best *(Crowd repeats)*
'Cause when you meet the best, you go down like all the
rest *(Crowd repeats)*
So be cool!

We're gonna take you higher *(Crowd repeats)*
We're gonna light your fire *(Crowd repeats)*
So get on up and get on down *(Crowd repeats)*
Let's move their team all around *(Crowd repeats)*
Blow your whistle woo, woo *(Crowd repeats)*
7-6-5-4-3-2-1, now get up XX, come on, come on get up
 XXX *(Crowd repeats)*

Are you ready? (yeah)
Are you ready? (yeah)
Well let's go (2, 3, 4)
We're gonna fight (2, 3, 4)
We're gonna win this game tonight

Don't need a turkey (NO)
Don't need a goose (NO)
Cause we Eagles (YEAH)
Stay on the loose (YEAH)
We are the Eagles (YEAH)
We know we're bad (YEAH)
Cause those Turkeys (YEAH)
Just been had (YEAH)

In Review

✓ Your job as a cheerleader is to direct the crowd's attention to your team.

✓ Your voice is your most important means of communication; take care of it. When necessary, use a megaphone or a microphone.

✓ Discuss your game plan in advance with the songleaders and other spirit squads.

✓ Orchestrate your cheers with appropriate hand, arm, and leg movements.

✓ Embellish jumps with different arm and leg poses.

✓ Partner stunts add flair, variety, and a touch of the dramatic to a routine.

✓ Cheerleaders often use tumbling techniques; however, you must master these stunts thoroughly before you incorporate them in your routine.

Photo Credits

Scott Smith took most of the photos for this book. The other photographers whose works appear here are: *page 5 (except bottom right)*, Sheila Graham; *page 6*, Rusty Tucker, DAILY BRUIN, UCLA; *page 8*, Ken Goodman, DAILY BRUIN, UCLA; *page 32*, Doug Gray; *page 33 (left)*, Wayne Levine; *page 35*, Nathan Faulkner; *page 36*, Curt Ensign, DAILY BRUIN, UCLA; *page 39 (top)*, Nathan Faulkner; *page 41 (top left and bottom)*, Nathan Faulkner; *page 50 (top)*, Sheila Graham; *page 70 (top)*, Sheila Graham; *page 75 (top left and bottom)*, Sheila Graham; *page 75 (right)*, Robert Taylor.